tether

tether

Brent Cantwell

RECENT
WORK
PRESS

tether

Recent Work Press

Canberra, Australia

Copyright © Brent Cantwell, 2023

ISBN: 9780645651317 (paperback)

A catalogue record for this book is available from the National Library of Australia

Cover image: Greg Wilson via unsplash

Cover design: Recent Work Press

Set by Recent Work Press

recentworkpress.com

EF

for my family
Amy, Harvey, Cerys and Mena

Contents

place of shelter

crossing the fault

anywhere-Pacific

place of shelter

a picture of Erena Pareraukawa

out of nowhere specific, a picture:
eyes rippling sideways always shore-ward
your still-water still-sometimes ta moko,
our tipuna, a face in the water
then my uncle speaks of stern Hokima—
your father—making a vessel of you,
'cause I see how before steadies
the wood and korowai of your shoulders
with a tarred line in a cabbage tree bay
sheltered enough
                              to cross the fault
between us, where plate tectonics
shift, where the slow smoke
of some other ship shimmers your Louis
shore-ward, a mainstay, my uncle assumes
because across such distances
marriage and tremors are indistinguishable,
so—ever the historian—he speaks
in understatements: musket wars, whaling
a culture of reciprocity ...
                              unstoppable lines
holding—somehow—this star waka steady
enough to house and hold your tamariki—
eleven by my uncle's count—and I
don't know how these slow continents
tether as they grind, grind as they tether;
bow of mana tethering the mana of your bow,
all I know is from this anywhere-Pacific—
steadied by the tarred lines of before and between—
you cut the sea's familiar unknown

Memorial Wall, Caroline Bay

for my sister

when my sister was ripping her way into the world,
we were stuck down the bay:
a darling harbour, before dawn, fog-undone

Dad parking up, my brother and me preparing
crenellations, pa and mana
with a red and yellow bucket and spade

dividing the sea and the shore
as remembering
draws a line in the light—

there was a squat Memorial Wall at Caroline Bay
but it didn't help much—
at each end, a granite-grey ball rough as wet sandpaper—

actually, the loss-marbles of grandparents helped:
Amiens, Passchendaele, Thiepval—
they were magnets to my three-year-old knees—

when I skipped the first full stops of a violent century
I tripped,
cutting a bloody trench of my own in the sea

and because memory rips to stick like birth
revealing a red-emerge morning
on a scraped-knee day,

the best I can offer is a sheltered bay—

Moonee Beach

drift all you like Moonee Beach—
tomorrow sand-wind will dune a new coincidence
and a family might come—

families might clump together sea-weed happy, or not,
or jelly-fish free—
impatient parents might say, *have some bloody patience*—

sons might stomp the sand boulders of crabs—
land-crab dads might shoulder-red their faces with beer—
a girl might find a specimen for her bucket—

her grandad might call it *a microcosm in a microcosm*
and he'd be right—
today every mother will say, *this is a special place*

because tomorrow will be different—

Pleasant Point Jan '83

when was another indifference
you think The Point was *the place?*
we opened our eyes under water:
leaf, used band-aid, comb—the misplaced

things cold-wet time makes of us—
were evidence in the mire
of day-deepening densities
so we were of swing-rope-an'-tyre

we were the plunge-butterflies
the stench of the dank-bark-rot to come
the past taking over
green-o'-weeping-willow green of the sum

total of our endless-summer splash
strangler-weed at *m' ankies*
because *before* leaves sticks,
stones, clods, car keys,

broken bark and boar-bones,
brown bottles
forgotten in Dad's river-fridge,
Le-Tan, discarded yogurt-pottles

with no use-by-date-and-time!
you still think The Point was *the place?*
open your eyes-under-water:
not one leaf, used band-aid or comb is mis-placed

ten years old

until I'm rhythm in this mud
until my knees are kicked-dirt dry
and grey, and the fence is a thud
and a ball feathers the sky

until my charge of cheap thunder
is silkiness unstoppable,
there'll be no place to stand under
where I can feel clean water fall

the brittles

some mornings—
most mornings come July—
by the boat place,

where the frost-frayed corner of Evans Street
and Grants Road
turned our damp-ambling school-ward,

puddles formed and froze
where pieces of pathway
petered

where me and my brother
removed the woollen mittens our Nana knitted
and smashed the ice that formed

pre-dawn in what we called the brittles,
or I did later
when I needed a metaphor for poetry

when I couldn't shake out the ache,
the cold hum knelling in the knuckles
of a dumb fist

I was looking already for *another* puddle,
another mood of mud
knowing every flippant twist of dirty water

might fall again to the brittles,
to the intricate prison of noun and shape,
to the cold chance of form on a morning of glass

red tin shed

heading back
a few tent pegs short
we ditched
the canvas chairs.
Last night's fire
left a moraine of its own:
a charred patch
set in a circle of stones;
the rough vowels
of a dry throat;
the hack of the axe
we left behind.
But the red tin shed
makes no sense!
It fits a map
below the skin,
the calendar
of a less sheltered coast
where slow boats
list still
and recede
like each day's
hard actual ice
leaving whalers,
run-holders,
botanists
and geologists
always
heading back

remembering the Ben Venue

on Waimataitai Beach, rock-hopping now
and then, trying to turn
the stony space beneath the cliffs and the sea
into 'pitiless shingles' again,
finding what is left of the 'moorings'
finding 'paltry wood and iron'
eighty degrees to the ground
listing into another wash-away tide
bringing 'the bruised and shattered bodies
of men and women' shipped-ashore

ashore now, into the present now,
re-tensing tarred lines,
steadying *then* enough for one more rescue
before 'the cables holding the *Ben Venue* part ... '
before the memories of salt-sprayed men
'turn[ed] broadside'
and 'capsize [d]'
beneath an as yet unnamed cliff
so 'over a thousand spectators'
can curtsey the safe-now dream of a once 'barbaric' coast

Hydro Hotel, Timaru

I'm tethered to this place
because elegance, or the taste of cigarette smoke
on a faux-mink throat, facades decay *husky*
and, surreptitious, the old lady on the hill
fag-hands her swing-door wide
and I clock her new coat but say nothing.
With too-bright art-deco lips, she welcomes me
as she welcomes *them off the boats* for a few
and eventually we lean on polished pine
polishing off your jug then mine

and if the chat remains phatic in the low-light
of *this weather we're havin'*
or *is your family well?*
if the paua-shell pool-table light
swings tarred lines to ambiguity-enough,
you might not even have to
surreptitiously back out of the room
on the mainstay of a clause,
on the lost buoyancy of an ill-conceived turn:

that I'm tethered to this place
like I am tethered to the shadow-rooms
of bad poetry
the silent smoke of a contagious corner
the say-nothing loud of being ashore
and drinking alone.
I love it here *because* of the bad poetry
because I'll never know what you truly mean,
just that you mean what you say.

the Caroline

in 1836—some say—
the Caroline haunted a sheltered bay,
a Sydney barque emerging out of the mizzling
out of this other prison
out of the wind-misted other-world of the sea

the sodden creak of joints and dead-tree wood
the bark-crack of no-one speaking,
all watching,
watching the sea-dog lick of a surface
the grey-green under or beyond

hungry for the dry bread of a sack
as hungry as the sea
nibbling at the singing shingles,
a red tin shed almost making sense
and the *come-ashore* of a clay-yellow cliff

what hope was there in a port-taut rope?
no one remembers these half-men whole—
these men ashore—
they haunted a sheltered bay
in 1836—some say—
calving an end on the end of a harpoon hook

some Rakaia

because it was warm,
he wore his gumboots
without socks
though they squelched—
lung-black—
making a wet cough
of walking
and at the top—
near the bulge of his calf—
a red ring
formed the last red scar
of the kiss
that kept
the rubber taut
and they were easy
to pull on
when he wanted milk
for coffee,
and the service station
on the highway
was close,
but most of all
he could walk
the side-road edge
then down the middle—
smoke on his lips—
lost
in some Rakaia

at Tunnel Beach

he wears one of those *hippy* necklaces—
he probably bought it in a tourist shop
by Tunnel Beach—
it clings to the jut of a shouldered bone
as he clings to the jut of a shouldered bone—

his skin is wet-sand still to touch—
not *like* wet sand,
erosion's wind-swept souvenir—
the wind that erodes this granite crag
erodes the pores that cry *time goes by*—

his hair is pulled back into a dry tangle
of un-kept kelp—
he wants to braid the nonsense of the sea
into the crag-shadows of Tunnel Rock—
he wants to be Tunnel-Rock still,

clinging to the jut of the shouldered bone
of a slow southern spine—

the old men of Waimaitaitai

The old men of Waimataitai live in plaster-board flats now
staring out of alcoves,
cracked old-man elbows polishing chair-arms hard
and they laugh, and grumble too, and speak as lava flowed to the sea:
a tacit memory of pahoehoe
forging *whaddaya* and *do some bloody work why don' ya!*

It is the stop-cold growl of the hot-slow stir:
his *mum on a flu cart, dad out o' work,*
empty stomachs rumbling town to town with *a gut full o' typhoid,*
and Roy, Roy'd had *a gut full o' war* by the time things cooled down
and now, now he's *garn out looking for trouble,*
now he's *up to his neck in no-good.*

But, it's OK, it's a place of shelter:
you can see their wrinkled lines and strata,
you can see men-of-stone clenching their fists
to work a pumice-heart free.
The old men of Waimataitai speak as lava flowed to the sea
grumbling in the margin of 'the great stone book.'

magpie mind

There are fenced-off houses there now.
The paddock
we cut through once to get to school—
the black pine-row
and grey-mystery ditch—
is residential parking now
and only empty during the school run.
Forty's a funny sort of above.
Now I stop
on the fence I used to hop
to beak-sort the dumb nut of now
from the dried kernel
of way-back-then.
This is pinecone-love
to a magpie mind:
I still jump the pine-wood stile.
I still warm my feet in a cowpat
and hurry past the brown-weight of a cow.
I haven't forgotten the bog-lost shoes,
the horse-nipped shoulders,
dead creeks turgid with negotiations
but now, I swoop and sail
and weigh the past on a pine-cone scale.

staying on the mountain

Feet barely in the ground, my son and I
find a tree lying in a patch of fern gone wild.
Seeing a knotted knuckle of dirty roots, he smiles:
an unclenched fist ripped from a mountain's side.
Looking up at me, he asks, *did you hear it fall?*
It fell two nights back, muffled to a feather in a dream
but loud enough, so I say how it seems
we hear every tree that falls.
Not a din of splinters or the up-heave of clods and roots,
but a punch-in-reverse, the surrender-now of leaves.
Then, panicking, as if the deafening timbre of *timber*
could be muffled to a feather in a dream,
he asks, *will we stay here, Dad?*
and I surrender, from root to leaving, as usual *yes.*

crossing the fault

crossing the fault

for Rita

When I crossed the strait alone
the way you shade an edge
to show a secret falling away,
I got talking to a man in a charcoal suit.

At first, he clutched a suitcase against his chest.
I noticed a frayed sleeve, coal dust petering,
and leather straps flapping—at least—a grey-sea sound
for the understatement of his heart.

Later, his suitcase on the ground,
a long-neck bottle-of-beer enough
to pencil-sketch a confession,
he traced to my eye the sad line of his life.

But when I crossed the fault later alone
noticing a little rip in the land,
it felt like bad things were happening
because no one spoke,

because the grinding under-grey of the plate
was left unmarked.
I *just* wanted someone to say something,
to smudge a piece of the world against a piece of the world.

Aoraki Moraine

After our still-frozen blueberries
manuka honey and oranges pealed,
there was a drift of smoke between you and me

an unfelt drift of smoke in a field
of cold toes trekking snow-tussock Aoraki
where—heavy with silt—a lake of wet steel

revealed the long shadow of a five-crag valley
and we chanced a look at what *there* remained:
colossal dice tossed free.

Later we were told they were the moraine
what was left behind when a glacier recedes
when a *valley* clears its throat of names.

I remember you clearing your throat with the need
to talk but I don't recall your advice
or how your hand felt in mine, or our need

to know what would be left when the drift of *us* cleared:
a memory of a time that was   *nice* ...
of blueberries not thawed   that we feared
we would never break this ice.

head injury

I am lying with what I have.
The bed—the concrete path by Room 2—is made up:
a pillow from the reading mat,
a blanket from Sick Bay.
I feel like I am sketching my school back from the bay.
I can even see the scruffy pot of pencils shading the white window sill
grey.
But the concrete's silver, the lunch bench wet
and I screw up my paper face
half-darking the crease and the fold of each sentence
until no-one is saying 'don't run in the rain'
anymore.

on Placa Reial

Currency's the current that flows between us
on Placa Reial.
On stone-stopped sheets bargains bob salmonella sticks,
lighters and flies.
Enormous smiles buoy us down boulevards,
rippling new diversions, and that's OK.
Tourists mark tides with collapsed umbrellas
so the rapids—
the *my-frien'-my-frien'-my-frien'-my-frien'*
and all that jazz—are easily sluiced
'til a man with no umbrella
drags a dead note from a river tapping an under-toe—
tap-tatap-tap tap-tatap-tap
a syncopation below the surface,
stone-rhythm-need—
on Placa Reial we just don't know when
we are crossing these dried-up river men.

night bus, Neasden

It was the mid-winter stir,
the plum-dark walk home,

the pre-work murmur
outside the façade of a cafe

where buses stop.
It was the on-your-way-ness of January

looking side ways
at low-whistled smoke,

smoke sent to the smog-light of Neasden.
But most of all,

it was the slowing-creep
of his five o'clock shadow

that coaxed him to an empty bus,
taut as a pin,

self-consciously
poised for one last groove home.

Worn vinyl crackles
as the needle slides silently to its seat.

hospital update

My son's lot park their cars fast and ignore
the weight of the drive in their boot steps.
I can hear them flutter *nothing-to-do* corridors,
demanding updates, moths of *whatever-light-is-left!*

The other lot bang on windows after hours,
the cold-fire flicker of *always-there* screens
wanting, like their parents, updates too, just not ours.
I like to think that my lot, in a roomful of teens,

might fly in the calm light of an *always-open* window.
But we don't, we fluster at glass, wanting just one more
update, a moth sounding at least life-wet, the same slow
more-moth thumbing, cars parked fast, and slammed doors

against children and grandkids leaving me hating
as I leave because everyone except me is updating.

beggars in Florence

Outside, the broken-brickwork of Santa Maria del Carmine
reveals the strata of shoulders housing *Masaccio's Expulsion*,
as well as the rag-prayers of the nameless.

Inside, there are ruins, thrusted-loins, helpless thieves in sheep-skins,
vast arches of grey conquered skies
ribbing sacred-hearted key-stones in time.

Everyone else is hunched back to a harvest in Africa,
a slow calendar in the skin,
carried now on murder cycles, crippled inside now,

outside begging for junk, everyone's miraculous junk!

locked-in

On the ward, the sway of you
reaches
out to us from the night-shadows
of a sterilizing
moon. Bareness and corridors suggest
branches
so you look to the window
blind
'cause window blinds open
traps. Pruned
you are paleness.
There's two of you
left. You are
the crudity of chiaroscuro:
an angel in a night-gown
or a crazed spinster dragging
a drip-frame
'round the ward
a squeak at midnight
a mouth gaping
the not-barking between us
of trapped sap.

a tourist in San Sebastian

a bus on a bay of glass is just
a scratch—
and we listen to our guide scratch the surface:
cessations, cease-fires, separations—

the scratch of a kiss in the morning moon is just
a scratch—
a hyphen's just a scratch,
a scratch for names so names need not surrender:

San Sebastian-Donostia—
you-me—
the other side of your quivering thigh, San Sebastian,
incompletes Donostia, and me—

we don't kiss in the bar-window light—
our bodies don't know how to be rough with love—
we turn the same face to the same moon,
a tourist *or* a terrorist—

the blood of heaven blooms car-steel, fire and flesh—
a rose by any other name is just a scratch—

magnolia

Sometimes—when the off-home ghost
of a too-clean life

is just too clean to play *the wife*—
I go to a cheap hotel down the road

and attempt—with lipstick and red wine—
a mid-week check-in.

I love the lamp-dust desperation
of half-lit receptions,

cigarettes left in ashtrays,
cheaply-painted euphemisms.

I love the polite *hellos* that are smiles
thrown hopeful

down magnolia corridors,
the half-caught after-sound of a pub

and I listen—as strangers listen—
for the fall-to-the-wall,

the tumble-upstairs of something *casual:*
ah, magnolia,

the colour of the pause
before we close our doors.

health and safety

1

We were told to form a semi-circle
around the luggage bay of the bus
to guard against *eruptions*,
the *inevitable eruptions*
of *poor people, addled people, transitory people*,
the seismic migrations of *other people;*
and once suggested to the blood
we looked at streets over shoulders—for a while—
listening to the rhythm of the clenched stone:
La Rambla, rumbler, rumbling deep belly smells from the grate
in a gust of heat slowing our gust of *just-arrived* and *everything-to-do!*
Yes, La Rambla, something *is* about to happen—isn't that the point of you?

2

our guide's last health warning was *line your stomachs*
and when *we* all met him at nine he was Tom again
and everything was free-poured:
some of us found ourselves behind bars—in bars—
talking and drinking as lava flows
some of us danced on hot concrete because it was 4AM
some of us met men
and the girl I loved walked home alone
knowing Barcelona would be lost if there was any other thought in her head—
or in mine—
so *we* crushed more mint against the day's hard actual ice,
dreaming of the dark flow home flow intermittent flow La Rambla

a Christchurch to Timaru run

because it is quiet
because words
are often lost
to the rattle
of half-rolled-windows
and the blare
of a tape deck
a-couple-o-beers in,
I begin
to notice
between us
the slowly-shifting
spine
of the Southern Alps,
a jagged plate
nuzzling
beneath
a jagged plate
pushing foothills from the plains,
the foothills of a mumble
of a wheel-tap
a look-my-way
through
the crunching
gravel-song
of silence,
and I wait,
I wait for the greywacke weight
of words

to come
on a Christchurch
to Timaru run

gated community

Knocking knowing you don't feel well
children run slippery up non-slip stairs
to a new story and a new smell
which we feel compelled to tear

into rhyme and reason but you don't have
to open the door. The security
here is excellent. We can eat the pav
and cream when the strict brutality

of hot concrete has saved your shaking frame
when the pool has tanned your body for men
when indifference has cooled you with a swim
when codeine has dreamt you a Goddess again

chlorinated free of hair and smell
knocking knowing you don't *feel* well.

passing through

one scorched-desert June
just out of wilderness-Meknes
goat-head Meknes
jaundice-walled Meknes
from a crowded train
shunting red
from the coast,
Younis—
a metallurgist
from Chefchaouen –
stops
to pour tea
into tinted glass cups
and it's not a question
of courtesy—
pressing palms,
smiling each other's
hellos—
it's an answer
to transience,
the rising aroma
of strangers
passing through,
the deepening sepia
of a memory
already
swirled in a tinted glass cup

Marrakesh in the morning

before the day-camels
and the blazing white places
before the tooth-picked garlic snails
and the balconies of gin

a Bedouin boy
sweeps again last night's
blown sand from his father's
air-conditioned stall again

he has an old Yamaha
he knows will get him to Paris
'cause his father
insists, *you'll never get it going!*

Marrakech has horizons
like everywhere else:
some see a wall of red clay
in a garden of blood oranges

some wake at dawn and sweep
the sand at the edge of the sky

a boy in the toi-toi!

You play in the toi-toi
in a mood of mud,
a right angle
against a wrong green fence.
Your *siblings* show me skateboard knuckles,
grazed to the bone,
the intricacies of ripped skin
that *you* should—
everyone loves a scar!
But you sit there
adjacent to the complacency
of other kids
with one of those little pink books—
a new one—
writing
downhill
in the wind
and the speed
of a deliberately injured
syntax
on the bone-white knuckles
of the moon,
an inconstant moon
that should—
but it doesn't matter anyway!
How I read you
will be the under-reed
of the toi-toi now,
and the should-green of growth—

sharp as the flick
of a carpenter's tape—
will plume the blond after-shavings
of a freshly planed two by four.
I am only sorry
for how I read you
now you are writing *me*
watching
you—a boy—
play in the toi toi.

Eagle Heights afternoon

for Amy

the white paint in our garage
flakes from the cupboard handle
and the stool's leg like a marriage
revealing—through lacquer and scandal—

the slow-grown grain of a Summer Red
or Rose Gum: we've had so many days
here each Saturday-sentence is said
in the in-and-out-of-earshot way

we listen to the radio on the stool;
the kids are meeting mates,
or heading down to the pool
and distance ripens happiness as fate

nectars summer-buds honey-and-no-fuss
on weekends there are bees between us

night lights, Amsterdam

You were always *seeing me there later*.
By the time you arrived at Grand Centraal
there were too many Dutch angles—bicycles
cars, trams—and buildings with hooks. The canal

was already oil, a trick of densities
in the lamp-light: Vermeer of milk. Van Gogh
of a thousand candles. Frank. I'll see you
wherever light is allowed. But the blood-flow

beneath a well-wrought bridge?
The darker paint of *later* beneath a neon sign's
pink ol' Roxy muck o' fuzz?
A dreg-heavy head full of hard lines?

At Grand Centraal *you* see *me* way too late.
I'm mixed up in shadows that *just won't wait*.

liking a song, now

here in Algeciras it feels good to be—*like*—
perched on the wrist of the world at night

in a grey hotel. Our balcony's—
like—held up by *the Pillars of Hercules*

but below, unconcerned with time, it's us
but precarious   the couple we—*like*—sussed

out ages ago still drinking tequila
and talking all night there   we are made o'

glass   we rhyme everything we know
through the tint and salt of *por qué coño no*

sarcasm cuts as cut-lemons cut
not like light slicing a stained-glass heart

but now, it feels good to be—*like*—
perched on the wrist of the world at night

in a grey hotel reminded of a time and a song
and tomorrow's first fingers circling moist upon

the lip-stick-smeared wine-glass rim
we listen to a future we would like to sing

seeing you again in Santorini

Unexpectedly seeing you again in Santorini. Just saying *good to see you*. Sitting on the edge of the shallow end. Testing the water. The chlorinated syntax of a reheated ease—our dive in Kortula.

So, a bunch of us went to the beach. Without another word. We played Twister waiting for the bus. Your body *suggested* a shape—susurrus. The curved back of a shore line's
broken morpheme print-black sand. Volcanic. An
under-eruption.

Reaching bodies in the early surf, sub-
merging a silent clause because a body answered a body's happy-
pressure questions

the only grammar touch.

relative train ride to Monte Carlo

it doesn't much pay to pay much attention
though sometimes carriage doors don't shut:
we see train-loads of people speeding past us speeding past

we see all of our directions
we see the violence of our closeness
we see sleepers at a thousand frames per second

and because we are certain of only one stop,
old men waiting in stations seem stationary,
the pitted skin of a granite crag

and even the mustard-past of an old chateau on a hill
seems precarious
because of distance and speed and the luck of ascension.

But unclosed doors open and everyone's heavy with badges:
Armani, Gucci, Chihuahua and cocaine, darling,
darlings of density taking *their* time, with such singularity

we are dragged along to event horizons
of white yachts and crystal flutes, Moet in platinum buckets,
leather gloves for him, iced manicures for her,

diamonds from Africa, blood of the earth,
cigarettes that don't kill you, cases of Delamore 42,
future harvests, relative commerce, even light …
it doesn't much pay to pay much attention.

The Hermitage Hotel, Aoraki

There's a place for us on a broken plateaux
and there'll be no movement 'til we're told
...*yeah, right the Hooker Valley'll not blow...*
The tussock's a disturbance of gold.

There's a place for us in a recently booked hotel.
The turn-offs are clearly marked with an
...*under them mountains there   hell...*
and the sight of a flaccid thumb's tradition.

There's a place for us with a seismic kind of view.
...*the sheets'll be creased...* winks the manager's missus
actually saying, ...*staking your claim?*   too
though we're slate-panelled walls of heavy promises.

We lay—or will lie—in a hotel looked back on—
or forward to—on always-shifting ground.

getting to work

By the motorway end of Jellicoe Road,
behind a Smithfield Freezing Works truck
then a Datsun—a trade-in—destined for town,
past the granite tide there—by and by—
and the on-and-on of the sea
curving the cold weight of a cold shoulder,

you get to work on your ten-speed—
lagooning—a curved spine at a stop sign:
white socks, clipped and tight;
y' stubbies a lazy beige with a firm belt;
a tightly knitted tie tucked into a shirt.
An arm signalling—in good time—a turn.

And—by and by—'cause no one holds a lane
like a Dad, I watch you
ready your foot for the push
waiting for a gap to reveal itself in the traffic
and—for a blink—I lose you to a ute
and I am afraid

feeling temporary-about-myself afraid
through the sleeve-smudged simile of a window.
I don't feel hair-in-m'-face three
or cold-floor-morning four or—by and by—
the condensation of being thirteen
growing heavy through net curtains.

Instead I wonder if I am *like* you—
by and by—as I ready my foot for the push,
as I signal a turn on a ten-speed,
curving the cold weight of a cold shoulder,
motorway end of Jellicoe Road—not like you!
This is the way *I—like*—get to work.

casualties

gravel grating roof un-
zipping
half a cabbage shaken
in a pot—
the last wheel-jerk of the mind:
dad's gonna kill me—
daddy—
the buzz-dull sound of insects—
nothing to be done—
       but the reporter's there
       eyeing casual
       angles
dragging some body's
last intimate
moment
       to the middle-of-the-road:
       sad-attractive-young-female!
wondering if
       HIGH SPEED CAR CRECHE
       or the *reckless-teenager* tag
is going too far—
       iodine is applied
       to gravel-ripped edges—
a body's swabbed clean
       cut by cut—

*

turned on at six
the news establishes today's casual-
ties early—
you won't remember her name—
you will be half-drunk by the time
she's back at yours—
there will be anticipation
though it's a done deal—
it will be emphasized
that youth and beauty
make tragedy much,
much worse
that attractiveness bleeds
across so many frequencies
and you will only know her after
she's gone
viral—

an understatement

before my brother's 21ˢᵗ
we stood in circles
around quiet fires
and there were
a couple of guys
I remembered
from school
but now I was at *university*
and so many said it
in that buried
other way
like something
shifting
underground
thrown
to sarcasm's
slow silt
a dislodged rock
rubbing against
another dislodged rock
and because
I over-thought it
or perhaps
I under-thought it,
we had little to say
until out of nowhere specific
a real tremor!
and we *both*
realised

plate-tectonics shift!
and nodding back
my understatement
I started with
'did y' feel that?'

the Sounds

by the time we entered the strait,
we had two kids but weren't married
and—of course—Te Moana-o-Raukawa was rough as
but the Sounds—

the Sounds told us that the ground once shook,
that the fault cragging this place perfect
looked from above like the un-fury of frayed-knot
nature—

closer though, from the front deck of the Aratere,
I kept one good eye on my kids
and a clag of bracken holding together a broken rock,
my new-grey bones, if I'm honest—

it must have been early for me,
I was green
and either missing the blond flick of a toi-toi plume
or my daughter sucking on a teething husk—

a seal pup *doing the worm*
down a slippery rock into still-water who-knows-where,
or my son,
lost in the ripple of his own excitement—

I remember feeling so much was at stake there
and my daughter, barely walking,
leaving a broken biscuit on the edge of a plate,
stumbled my way, saying *daddy*—

I trembled then at the beautiful sound of *our fault*

anywhere–Pacific

arachno-naut

This morning
from a shady cabbage tree
to the bare branch
of our garden's
weeping willow
a spider—
with a plum-ripe abdomen—
assumes
a way
on self-shat silk
sticky with intent
defying gravity and distraction, swimming into space,
a joyful
anywhere-Pacific dream
of leaf-and-bark
and flying sacks of nutrition,
not ever
arriving
'cause arriving
is to know
the fall
and breath
of your own weight,
to spin a line fool enough to stop

a wake

Years in, we know *this* is the way to wake
at first light, when a splash-and-leap
breaks the blind-white surface of sleep;
a swimming thing in a volcanic lake

gets up, gets out of being under
deaf-rumbling. There's cloud too, a lazy sheet,
a sky-grey gap for feet,
for the morning's half-heard thunder.

On the lake, light—soft as wattle pollen—
ducks under as fish-out-of-water
leap—with tired eyes—out. We caught the
wake as we woke, soundly written:

not a perfect rhyme on still water
not an exact image carried out on
flat-water shoulders—but a cool shiver
now! easy accident-us on doubtful sounds

where lake-weed fingers fall to clinging
scanty, clad of a happy rock,
where the tumble-still of last night's lost blossom
is left—barely audible—to rhythm,

to the blab of the wave, to graphite-grey sticks
rippling always shore-ward on a compromised rhyme.
This is why bodies—'writ in water'—chime
a wake on *this* lake linguistic.

a standard candle

as you turned thirty,
we grew apart: I wanted you to
move into a box-room in Willesden Green, but you wanted to go
away travelling, lounge alone in another square somewhere far
from the
light of a standard candle,
its blinding routines, its magnolia-bland mornings, your
apparent *wanna-get-out-of-the-room* evoking in me such
intensity—pulsar-lighthouse on the cliff-edge of
how-could-you?—you shielded your eyes from the
bright-ness, and earnestly intoned, *as we move away from light*
its apparent intensity—how bright it
looks—will decrease in proportion to the square of the distance
Willesden far away now—a doubled distance—my apparent brightness
decreased by a factor of four, then,
in Kortula, we talked on the phone of
proportions and infidelity, and I said you were
too logical, couldn't see things my way, from my angle, though
the distance tripled, apparent brightness down by a factor of nine, in a
square of honest vegetables and boxed up junk, you *could* see me, speaking
of courage and sunglasses, yelling now: *if you know*
the brightness—a standard candle—you can calculate the
distance

a local injection

after my extraction
I took the long way home
assuming—
like a blind fool—
the flat-noon of Ngaio
lunch
at a window
radish and cress
in a crockery bowl
the daily un-opening of books
the un-grey of garden leaves
a post-
man far-away
on a bike
still-ringing
so you know he's been
and always
will be
weather-bored
white weather-board
Ngaio,
you're the gap in my jaw now!
you're the empty space
I want to tap
to prove your backstreets still exist

gap year

what dreams
shunt you
idling
half past dark pipes
and disappointing
cables?
what faces
stitch repairs?
what beautiful
people
crumble apart
together
like newborn daylight
on smog
as soft as talcum
powder?
what garish
eyes
and blue
shadows
fill these desperate
laundrettes
with questions?
what
bright
residue
chases dead
lines down
non-descript

stares
to gaps
I don't mind?

Pax Romana

nudge-at taxis
  nudge tourist packs;
      of-pack tourists
         pack Rome's
Pax Romana
  of-freedom murder cycles
     whine beneath the of-weight
              of sabato
       a grit-glare sun
  glares down at of-cleavage streets
at of-slurp cigarettes
     this of-babble
        Babel
         gridlocked
     column-shocked
        squarking
          pigeon-english hawkers
           with muscle-through heads
             buoying
    an of-salt sea of *everywhere-to-go*
  and *nothing-else-to-do*
     beneath the of-throng mustard stone
        the hymn-shadowed
        salsa-cool
         Spanish steps

watching Dad taking his time on a walk

down you go
down the pine-row
word-row
gravel-track in a hat
bought back in the acronym
years ago
though today
you take time to stop and see the maggies
swoop
and when the coast's clear
you pick-a-pinch of mulberries with hard delicate fingers
so chickens, wild-on-sugar, lurch-and-peck and forget the weight
of an abbreviating
world
and you pick your nose
smiling
at the flippancies holding everything-together-long-enough
to resist the pull-
down
then you laugh out-loud because goats-*do*-have-beards
and before the sun is
down,
before the gum is done dappling every precious leaf light to no-light
and back
again
you wander back
again
up a pine-row
word-row

gravel-track
that looks to me—
way up here—
like the lazy line
of an easy abbreviation

left out

behind the diamond coach grinds an axe
to keen each *wasted afternoon*
to a disciplined edge   such control lacks
the mischief of distance   me a mere moon

away   left out field   watching a red 'n' white kite
suffer the plunge, the deep–blue of the wait,
not seeing an easy high ball and like
an axe   coach hacks *on y' bike, mate!*

to me   coach, the mitted and the boast
are no great tether to me a plan's like
spitting in the sea, strategy the ghost
of a sailor's hope, my *on y' bike!*

some people just want to be left out
to suffer the plunge and the doubt

leaves, leave!

(based on Marcus Skipper's Alan Marshall, 1995)

I know autumn should stop my boots with leaves,
leave me to hulk here like an old Falcon
in a field lost to rust, rust that eases
this red earth still, but still I am welcome,

welcome as a bird! my wings are sky-wide
pages pressed to the quick-breath of so
much nothing to yarn, and a sky so wide
leaves so little time and so much leaving still to do

dog whistle

Here I go again
hoicking a blast
on a dog whistle,
waiting for proof,
for Sue—
the loyal lab next door—
to leap a fence
on scuffed paws
on a feast
of crunched biscuits
wagging a curious tail
proving
this sound—
without cognate—
real.
But not today.
Sue does not come.
Assuming the worst,
I backwards-map
the contours
of lament,
slow-step
the gravel-crunch
of this who-knows-where
driveway,
this go-anywhere
of sound
and when I stumble
on a friend

and a dad
standing around
the place
where Sue
was placed—
her spine
gone
to the vibration
of some-other wheels—
I run away
not wanting to know
where *this* high blast
– just born—
may lead

chill-out rooms

After the dance—*big fish little fish*
put it in a box—we seek crepuscular
corners—chill-out rooms— to flesh out each foot
with words like *concupiscent muscular* ...

men submit to shape sweat salt 'n' sinew
in the half-light on a hot plate sizzling
everything that is possible in you
moving slower without thought out there in

the never-places where lip-stuck faces
pare treacherous words down to the iamb
a butterfly sits where my heart paces
I answer the pin   *I am who I am* ....

a poised lepidopterist bops and clocks
big fish little fish   put me in a box.

outside Te Anau

Sound is not quite asleep here.
Birds sing without pepper but they sing.
The salt and fat of *everywhere-to-go*
and *still-so-much-to-do* does not sting

the teeth to blind the tongue.
A tui twitters in the dark,
the midnight-heaviness of the dumb
meanders grass-ward and I mark

only an under-groan, and what may moo
but knows no ears or eyes.
I hear a car far-away. It might be you.
It might not. We know the whys.

Outside's dark-field rustling away when we
are locked-in to such low fidelity.

outside

outside's assumed through a fly-wire
in—
we assume the mountain—
the coast far   away
knowing this semi-permeable membrane
strips the hills of its under-
hum,
the wind of the sea's salt—
it's my way of leaving
a rake out—
it's my way of clawing this,
this ragweed-midnight—
it's my way of reaching out at the strangled possum sounds—
the moon-striped driveways—
a brush turkey
on a tin-roof somewhere
clawing at the ragweed—
probably-chickens
perch in the dark
clenching quills, like me—
clawing at the ragweed like me—
assuming
as the fruit bats of Sagganto Park
way
down
there
assume
absence-in-darkness
when the squeak of late-night barbequed meats

and halloumi cheese on the teeth
is heard no-more
though they shriek still
and claw
at this ragweed-midnight—
like me—

Turnpike Lane

Still, green and blind we follow the same sun
knowing it'll follow us, knowing it'll soon
go down on a hotel in town somewhere
on rows of shoulders shrugging off sixteen-hour
shifts, skulking home after a pint babbling
excited almost-somewhere-almost-accents.

Families dragged from Africa drag accents,
skin, the blood of the land beneath a new sun
where children clutch at yellow skirts babbling,
bulging grey not-my-sky eyes brought far too soon
to the buying of things, ocean-bound bags, hour
on hour, on buses red and heading somewhere.

Dark-denomed indian-summer nights somewhere,
men knawing on qat sticks, picking at accents
wanting taxi-cabs at 5am, the hour
of chewed cheeks and *plenty o' green* in the sun,
in the amber light of ... *is it morning soon?*
should we prepare to stop ... ? still our babbling

surfaces with sleep ... in bedsits babbling?
dry pipes ache at slept-through days because somewhere
wives wait for cheques, and men—that will send them *soon*—
yell *they is live like squatters here,* their accents
thicker, breaking at *m' son's back home,* the sun
drying the pipes, the ache of another hour ...

… but there's amnesia in distance and one hour
away dreams shunt us idling down babbling
tracks to disappointing cables and the sun
is forgotten, coverage lost and our somewhere
faces stitch repairs, search the fade for accents
and connect the topside disconnect with arriving soon:

a crowd crumbling together in the smog soon,
alighting in the late light! and such an hour
silhouettes, fades, blurs industry, age, accents,
pay scales, cell phone towers of babbling,
the calendar in our skin, a delay somewhere
aching down the line still lost 'cause every sun

will go down soon on the blues, the babbling
hours, the windows of hiss, a hotel somewhere
throwing accents back at the same old sun.

Strange Tides

for Aysun

This has nothing to do with the moon.
The moon provides light so we can see
hard lines on faces drawn hard too soon.

Four hundred thousand faces trying not to see
the crowded boats and the sickening-sway,
those quietly facing an unquiet sea.

No one tells the children *it'll be OK*.
There's no singing and no one's immune
to the fleeing, the huddling, the deciding, the sway

of the sea beneath the moon
where deciding, jumping, not-breathing, no fight
sways and has nothing to do with the moon.

On Ali Hoca Point beach there is no light.
The moon has *made it* West too soon
dragging another strange tide in without much fight:

beads, photos, phones, kelp,
plastic water bottles, a balloon,
papers, someone's son and no help.
Strange tides have nothing to do with the moon.

bloody excellent canopy

I asked around
but no one could tell me the species.
No one could even name the over-hanging knots
and dead-growth providing

the bloody excellent canopy before every beach
down this coast,
a cool moment's reprieve
from another bloody scorcher.

Someone must've planted this dry scratch
of a tree;
someone must've cut a rough path
or coaxed *a way* with pruning.

Or is this place of shelter un-tended?
a coincidence of boogie boards
and arse-cheek sand;
a child with blood-grit knees;

a dad burnt and buried in the shifting sand;
a mum squinting behind her sunnies
and the smoke-jut of her lips,
lathering lotion on the backs of her boys;

most of all, teenagers playing volley-ball
in the black-sand easy-mirror
of *almost out* ...
no wonder we blink blind on a beach

stepping from such a bloody excellent canopy

facing Uranus (Voyager II)

conduit of my eyes
forgive me
I could not face the distant sea

the endless stony shore
before the rivers
of gas

the poorly strung storm of some god-motif
collapsing
violin-like into liquid methane

a *book* I could face
but not the ultra-violence of heading out
in a carriage alone

package—for me—the gravity of entrance
the harvest
of a bagging hook I would not *like*

conduit of my eyes
forgive me
I can not *face* the *book* either

just the last dance, please,
the lulling turn of seventeen hours
the green hypnosis of milk

Voyager I, 14th Feb. 1990

(after Pale Blue Dot by Voyager I - Photo)

you are a butterfly in the stomach
of the plunge   you made it   —
astonishing—out of the Cape to
the pebbled shore of   some-
other-sea they said *you looked
back   one   last   time* but
it was better than just looking
back! you transmitted pixels
you trapped the light in a grain
of sand   you trapped the sea
in an old tin cup   and us! un-
tethered-us   on a planet
turning pale on a tide   but
you don't recognise   home
you don't see how distance
renders us   dust on a slice of
light as soft as talcum powder
that we sit in the pale-blue
Cape-light of February   in an
afternoon garden   beneath a
pignut close enough to kiss—
a kiss lost in the bat-black
shadow of being   alone
it is a connection only
you can capture six billion
kilometres   deep   we yearn
as you yearn from *our* absolute
edge   distance blurs *our*
nerves steel-cold too   we
are butterflies   in the
stomach of the   plunge—

dark-sky park

Campsite's paper-bark quiet.
Out there—the ghost gums.
My daughter—my first—
possums the way you do in a tent
when you're young and barely know where you are.

She finds a zip—realising.
She tears a wall telling me she can't sleep,
that the silence
and the cicadas out there
are shrieking white-wing wordless.

I hold her—of course—
in a single-splendid-movement-of-the-arm
and show her the April sky:
a black-noun canvas
white-silence knows where.

And when I pick my way from The Pot to Sirius,
a billion stars,
a billion light years away,
white-click *their* wings
sparking the same blip-blip endlessness.

And *I* tear a wall in the scattered-gas what-cloud
of a no-
noise nebula—realising:
we're too inside to really look out
from this single-splendid-movement-of-the-arm.

Notes

'remembering the Ben Venue' - All quotes rescued from *The Timaru Herald May 1882* (Sourced from, https://sites.rootsweb.com/~nzlscant/benvenue.htm) and https://teara.govt.nz/en/photograph/7291/the-ben-venue-and-city-of-perth

'the old men of Waimataitai' - From 'Notes on the Geology of South Canterbury' (1908) by John Hardcastle referring to his 'reading' of the Geology around South Canterbury in particular at Dashing Rocks near Waimataitai Beach where lava flowed from Mount Horrible/ Wapouri to meet the sea.

Acknowledgements

I wish to warmly thank Amy Clark for her support, patience and stamina, on and off the marathon trail.

Loving thanks to my friends and whanau who have shaped this collection. I am truly grateful. To my mum, Val Holden, for the photos, for a glimpse at our whakapapa and for teaching me the art of never saying goodbye. To my dad, Tony Cantwell, for always offering a big hello and the sound of thunder that tells me you're on your way.

Special thanks to the Cantwell, the Holden and the Clark families, for just being Cantwells, Holdens and Clarks. To my dear friends Stephen and Nicole Cain, may we always walk different paths up the same mountain.

To my dear children Harvey, Cerys and Mena who this is for, who keep me tethered.

I also wish to extend my deep gratitude to Shane Strange and Recent Work Press for believing in my book. And special thanks must go to Es Foong for offering fresh insights and generous feedback on my manuscript.

Lastly, I wish to thank the editors of the magazines and journals in which some of these poems have previously appeared: Tracey Slaughter, Denise O'Hagan, Emma Neale, Stuart Barnes, Gail Ingram, Erik Kennedy, Jeni Curtis, and Angela Gardner to name just a few. Your guidance and encouragement have made this collection of poetry possible.

'a sheltered bay', *Landfall vol. 235*, (2018), p. 23
'Pleasant Point, Jan '83', *Landfall vol. 233*, (2017), p. 74
'ten year old', Milly Magazine, 2019
'the brittles', *Landfall vol. 243*, 2022
'red tin shed', *Sweet Mammalian Issue 4*, (Spring 2016), p. 20
'the Caroline', *a fine line*, (Autumn 2022) ed. Gail Ingram
'some Rakaia', *Landfall vol. 240*, (2018), p. 62
'magpie mind', *Milly Magazine*, (2019)
'at Tunnel Beach', *Antipodes 3.1*, (June 2023)

'crossing the fault', New Zealand International Poetry Prize (3rd Place) NZPS Anthology 2022

'Aoraki Moraine', *Sweet Mammalian Issue 5*, (Spring 2017)

'night bus, Neasden', *London Grip*, (Spring 2017)

'health and safety', *Takahe 93*, (August 2018)

'a boy in the toi-toi', *Poetry NZ Yearbook*, (2022), p. 82

'Marrakesh in the Morning', *Takahe 90*, (2018)

'Eagle heights' (as 'bees between us'), *Takahe 102*, (2021)

'meeting me there later', *Foam: e Issue 16*, (2019)

'liking a song, now', *Foam: e Issue 16*, (2019)

'seeing you again in Santorini', *Mayhem 10*, (2022)

'always-shifting ground', *Turbine/ Kapahau*, (2016)

'getting to work', *a fine line, Autumn* (2022) ed. Gail Ingram

'casualties', *Meniscus Vol. 11 Issue 1*, (2023)

'the sounds', *a fine line, Autumn* (2022) ed. Gail Ingram

'arachnonaut', Milly Magazine (2019)

'a wake', *Takahe 102*, (2021)

'local injection', *Penquin Days*, (2016), p. 34

'Pax Romana', *Five2One Magazine*, (2018)

'left out', *Meniscus vol. 7 issue 1*, (2019)

'chill-out rooms' ('big fish little fish'), *Verge 2017 - Chimera*, (2017), p. 47

'outside Te Anau', *fresh ink voices reflecting on Covid-19 from Aotearoa New Zealand*, (2021), p. 90

'outside', *Australia Poetry Journal, Volume 11 Number 1—local, attention*, (2021), p. 41

'Strange Tides', *Blackmail Press 42*, (2017)

'dark-star park', *Takahe 103*, (2021), p. 29

'facing Uranus' (Voyager II), *Mimicry Issue 4*, (2017), p. 55

Voyager I, Cantwell, Brent, *Poetry NZ Yearbook*, (2021), p. 71

About the Author

Brent Cantwell was born in Timaru, South Canterbury on the East Coast of New Zealand's South Island. He received a Bachelor of Arts from the University of Canterbury in 1995 majoring in English Literature and History. After training to be a high school teacher, he moved to the United Kingdom where he spent five years teaching Drama and English in a London comprehensive. Always the travel diariest, he spent these years exploring and documenting the treasures of Europe, Africa and Asia.

On his return to the Southern Hemisphere, Brent settled in Wellington, New Zealand, where he and his partner Amy Clark had their first two children. After moving his family to Australia in 2011, first to Melbourne where their third child was born, then to Tamborine Mountain on the Gold Coast Hinterland, he began to seriously dedicate himself to writing poetry and short stories.

Brent Cantwell is currently teaching high school English on the Gold Coast and working towards his Masters of Creative Writing with Macquarie University. He has published poetry in a range of New Zealand and Australian literary journals including *Australian Poetry Journal, Poetry NZ, Landfall, Takahe* and *Foam:e.*

www.ingramcontent.com/pod-product-compliance
Ingram Content Group Australia Pty Ltd
76 Discovery Rd, Dandenong South VIC 3175, AU
AUHW020721050325
407891AU00005B/28